LIBRARY SERVICES	Maidenhead Library St. Ives Road Tel. 01628 796969		
W.I.D			

The Royal Borough

Windsor & Maidenhead

leisure & culture

CLASS NO. 759.04

TO AVOID OVERDUE CHARGES THIS BOOK SHOULD BE RETURNED ON OR BEFORE THE LAST DATE STAMPED ABOVE. IF NOT REQUIRED BY ANOTHER READER IT MAY BE RENEWED BY PERSONAL CALL, TELEPHONE OR POST.

17th Century Art

17th Century Art

PEEBLES ART LIBRARY   **Sandy Lesberg, Editor**

First published 1974
by
Peebles Press International
U.S.: 140 Riverside Drive, New York, N.Y. 10024
U.K.: 12 Thayer Street, London, W1M 5LD

ISBN 0-85690-029-X

Illustrations provided by:
Giraudon, Paris: pages 3, 9, 12, 15, 19, 21, 25, 28, 29, 30, 35 (upper),
36, 38, 40, 41, 46.
André Held, Lausanne: pages 7, 10, 11, 14, 16, 18, 20, 22, 23, 27, 31,
33, 34, 39, 42, 44, 45, 47, 48.
Bulloz, Paris: pages 8, 13, 17, 24, 37.
Archive Research, London: page 32.
Deutsche Fotothek, Dresden: page 43.

Distributed by
Walden Books, Resale Division in the
U.S. and Canada.
WHS Distributors in the U.K., Ireland,
Australia, New Zealand and South Africa.

Printed and Bound in Great Britain

Introduction

The 17th century is, if one thinks about it, the richest period in the whole history of Western painting from the point of view of the diversity and originality of the various schools. I say "if one thinks about it" because, in fact, if anyone is asked to name the most brilliant century in European painting the Quattrocento springs to mind, or the Impressionist period; not long ago one would have promptly said the 16th century. Nevertheless, the 17th century is the only one in which the five schools—Italian, Spanish, French, Flemish and Dutch— show equal outputs all at their peaks. (Eighteenth-century catalogues tended to refer to the " three schools" : Italian, French and Northern, the last embracing a mixture of German, Dutch and Flemish.) No school was completely dominant, as Italy was in the 15th and 16th centuries, and as France was in the 19th and first half of the 20th. It was a unique situation that all the European countries except Germany (though not forgetting the talent and importance of Elsheimer, who had a decisive influence on painters as different and as considerable as Rubens, Claude Lorrain and Rembrandt) created paintings which were very national in style and simultaneously on a completely international level.

In the preface to the last volume, I described the absolute importance of Rome as the 17th century's artistic capital. And this is true: no European painter existed who had not directly or indirectly, in person or through an agent, received, assimilated and exploited the lessons of Italian painting. Even more remarkable is the fact that in Holland and Spain the Italian culture accompanied the development of the two probably most strongly individual and eminently national European schools. At a later time there were to be minor Impressionists and Abstract artists in every country of the world. Usually, countries which do not currently have their own creative sources of painting copy, rather weakly, the dominant international movement; or else, under the illusion of preserving their originality, resist it and settle into a chauvinistic and sterile provincialism. But what, on the contrary, do we find in Spain and the Low Countries in the 17th century? We find Rubens, who grasped the very roots of the Italian "grand manner" in all its subtleties and turned them towards Flemish inspiration. We find Velasquez, nurtured by Titian and Raphael, but more Spanish than any isolated Spanish painter cut off from Rome could have been. Above all, we find Rembrandt, who never went to Rome, but whose art would be inexplicable without Caravaggio (none of whose pictures he can ever have seen) or without the whole movement of tenebroso *painting, which spread in Holland to establish one of its most influential centres, the Utrecht school, with the mysterious and poetic Ter Brugghen. Rembrandt, however, had nothing in common with what are called the " Caravaggisti", any more than Manet and Gauguin, the true descendants of Watteau, had with the later minor masters of the "fêtes galantes". The Spaniards and Dutch understood that it is never good to resist anything concerned with one's craft, but that one should be susceptible to all movements both within and without because mastery of them is the only way to liberate inspiration. We would have been spared many modern controversies around the schools of Paris, New York and Milan and the Cobra Group if artists had always understood that fear of influence paralyses creativity.*

About the mid-19th century, when modern painting was undergoing its great liberation, the Romantics, the Realists, and the early Impressionists suddenly experienced a prodigious stimulus from 17th-century Holland and Spain, one with its vast landscapes captured from real life and its unromanticised middle-class scenes, the other with its audacious colour, both with their still-life, in which fish, peaches and plums replaced the mythological heroes, great kings and saints of the Counter-Reformation. It is well known how much Courbet's cows owe to Potter's bull. Modern painters had the impression that *there* there was no more cheating. *" Titian and Leonardo da Vinci are swindlers!"* roared Courbet, justifiably. *" If either of those two came back to life and entered my studio, I'd take a knife to him. As for Mr. Raphael, he's not worth thinking about. But Ribera, Zurbarán, above all Velasquez—these I do admire."* [1] *This sanguine attitude, which was to lead to injustice to Italy described in my preface to the last volume, was a rather violent homage to those painters, both northern and southern, who had managed to become fully themselves without condemning those whose art differed from their own.*

Jean François Revel

[1] Reported by Théophile Silvestre in *Les artistes français*, 1861.

Harmenszoon Rembrandt van Rijn
Leyden 1606-Amsterdam 1669
Young Woman with an Old Woman
cutting her Toenails
Wood 10 × 8$\frac{1}{4}$ in.
Rennes Museum.

Murillo
The Melon Eaters
Pinakothek, Munich

Bartolomé Esteban Murillo
Seville 1617–1682
Virgin and Child
Palazzo Pitti, Florence

Frans Hals
Portrait of a Young Man, 1655-1660
Oil on canvas 25½ × 17¾ in.
Thyssen Collection, Lugano

Frans Hals
Boy reading
Canvas 30 × 24¾ in.
Reinhart Collection, Winterthur

Rembrandt
Venus and Cupid
Louvre, Paris

Rembrandt
Balaam's Ass
Musée Cognacq-Jay

C PABRITIVS 1654

Carel Fabritius
Haarlem *c.* 1620–Delft 1654
The Goldfinch, 1654
Oil on canvas, 13 × 8¾ in.
Mauritshuis, The Hague

Gerard Ter Borch
Zwolle 1617–Deventer 1681
The Military Gallant
Oil on canvas 26½ × 21¾ in.
Louvre, Paris

Rembrandt
The Jewish Bride, 1668
Oil on canvas 47¾ × 65½ in.
Rijksmuseum, Amsterdam

Rembrandt
Man in Turkish Costume
Pinakothek, Munich

El Greco
The Adoration of the Name of Jesus
(*Philip II's Dream*), after 1579
Oil on canvas 55 × 43¼ in.
Escorial, Madrid

El Greco
Portrait of Pope Pius V
Private collection, Paris

El Greco
The Wedding at Cana
Oil on canvas 11¾ × 16¼ in.
Strasburg Museum

El Greco
Crete 1547–Toledo 1614
Christ on the Cross with the Virgin,
St John and Mary Magdalene
Prado, Madrid

Vermeer
Street in Delft, *c.* 1658
Oil on canvas 21 ½ × 17 ¼ in.
Rijksmuseum, Amsterdam

Vermeer
Girl in a Blue and Yellow Turban, c. 1658
Oil on canvas 18¼ × 17¾ in.
Mauritshuis, The Hague

Velasquez
*Christopher Columbus presenting the
New World to the Catholic Kings*
Quimper Museum

Diego Velasquez de Silva
Seville 1599–Madrid 1660
Equestrian Portrait of the Duke of Olivares
Prado, Madrid

Velasquez
Las Meninas (*The Maids of Honour*) 1656
Oil on canvas 125¼ × 108¾ in.
Prado, Madrid

Velasquez
Portrait of the Infanta Maria-Margarita,
Daughter of Philip IV, c. 1655
Oil on canvas 27 ½ × 23 ¼ in.
Louvre, Paris

Adriaen van Ostade
1610-1685
The Schoolmaster, 1662
Oil on canvas 15¾ × 13 in.
Louvre, Paris

Gabriel Metsu
Leyden 1630–Amsterdam 1667
Woman peeling Apples, 11 × 10¼ in.
Louvre, Paris

Lely (Pieter van der Faes)
1618–London 1680
Henrietta of France, Queen of England, 1660
Oil on canvas 19¼ × 15¼ in.
Musée Condé, Chantilly

Frans Hals
Portrait of a Young Woman, 1655-1660
Oil on canvas 25½ × 17¾ in.
Thyssen Collection, Lugano

William Dobson
London 1610–1646
Naval Officer
National Maritime Museum, Greenwich

Francisco Herrera the Elder
Seville 1576–Madrid 1656
The Broom Seller
Oil on canvas 63 ½ × 43 ¾ in.
Musée Calvet, Avignon

Velasquez
Los Borrachos (*The Triumph of Bacchus*), 1629
Oil on canvas 65 × 90 ½ in.
Prado, Madrid

Francisco Zurbarán
St Lawrence
Oil an canvas 23 ¾ × 31 in.
Fine-arts museum, Cadiz

Velasquez
The Surrender of Breda (*The Lances*), 1635
Oil on canvas 120 ¾ × 144 ½ in.
Prado, Madrid

Francisco Zurbarán
St Bonaventure on his Bier
Oil on canvas 98 ½ × 88 ½ in.
Louvre, Paris

Francisco Zurbarán
Fuente de Cantos 1598–Madrid 1664
Adoration of the Shepherds, 1638
Oil on canvas 102 ¾ × 69 in.
Grenoble Museum

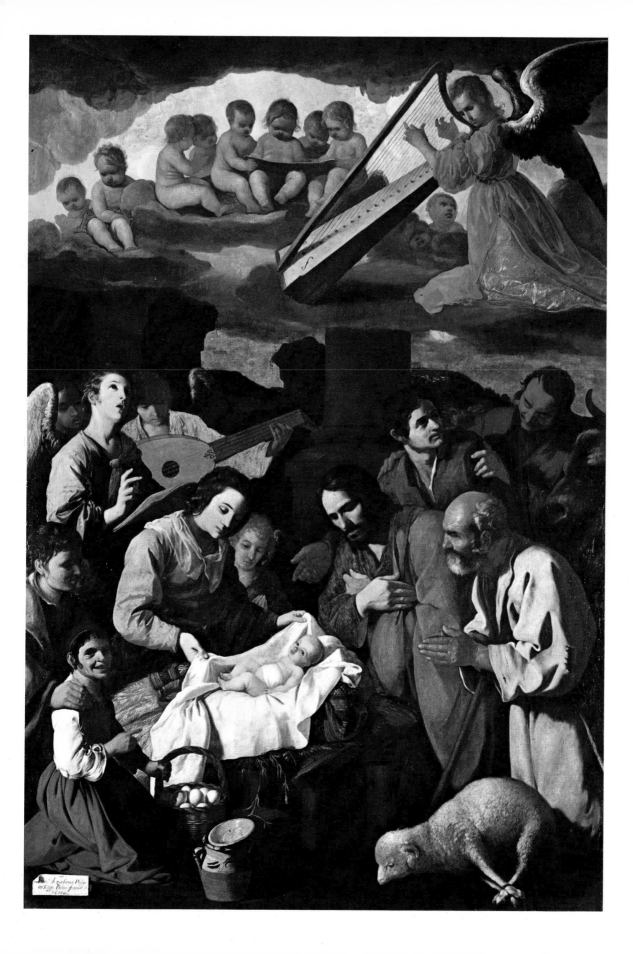

Pieter de Hooch
Rotterdam 1629–Haarlem 1684
The Card Players
Oil on canvas 26½ × 30¼ in.
Louvre, Paris

Frans van Mieris the Elder
Leyden 1635-1681
Portrait of a Young Lady, 1672
Oil on wood 12½ × 10 in.
Thyssen Collection, Lugano

Murillo
The Holy Family with a Little Bird
Oil on canvas 56¾ × 74 in.
Prado, Madrid

Gerrit Dou
Leyden 1613-1675
The Dropsical Woman, 1663
Oil on wood 32¾ × 26½ in.
Louvre, Paris

Vermeer
The Lacemaker, c. 1664
Oil on canvas 9 ½ × 8 ¼ in.
Louvre, Paris

Semion Fedorovitch Ouchakov 1626-1686
The Archangel Gabriel
Ikon
National Museum of the Monachal Convent,
Moscow

Vermeer
View of Delft, *c*. 1653
Oil on canvas 38 ½ × 41 ¼ in.
Mauritshuis, The Hague

Vermeer of Delft
Delft 1632-1675
The Love Letter, c. 1666
Oil on canvas 17¼ × 15¼ in.
Rijksmuseum, Amsterdam

Jacob van Ruisdael
Haarlem 1628-1682
The Shaft of Sunlight
Oil on canvas 32 ¾ × 38 ½ in.
Louvre, Paris

El Greco
El Espolio
Oil on canvas 72 ¾ × 49 ¼ in.
San Vicente Museum, Toledo

El Greco
The Burial of Count Orgaz, 1586
Oil on canvas 189 × 141¾ in.
Saint Thomas' Church, Toledo

Glossary of 17th Century Art

Aachen, Johann von (1552-1616)

German painter, born in Cologne, died in Prague. He assumed the name of the town of Aachen because his family came from there. Gifted with remarkable talent for design, he studied for six years with Jerrigh (a Flemish painter settled in Cologne), starting when he was sixteen. About 1574 he went to Venice and was deeply affected by Tintoretto. In Rome his pictures met with great success. He drew attention with a *Nativity* for a chapel in the Jesuit church, and established his reputation with his portraits of the celebrated musician Madonna Venusta and the poetess Madonna Laura. In 1588 he left for Munich, summoned by William V, Duke of Bavaria. There he painted a *Resurrection*, and *Helen, Mother of Constantine, discovering the True Cross*. The Emperor Rudolph II invited him to Prague, where he held his court. There the artist painted a picture of *Venus and Adonis*, with an elegance hitherto unknown in Germany and so successful that it earned him a definitive place in the Imperial Court. His *Bathsheba's Bath* (Vienna Museum) is generally considered his masterpiece.

Berchem, Nicolaes Pietersz (1620-1683)

Dutch painter, born in Haarlem, died in Amsterdam. His family originated in Brabant and emigrated to Holland because of religious persecution. His father, Pieter Claesz, was his first master, and he went on to study with Claes Mozaert and Jan Wils, whose daughter he married. In 1642 he became master of the Haarlem Guild. He went to Italy and painted pictures directly inspired by nature. When he returned to Holland he stayed a while in Haarlem, then settled in Amsterdam from 1677. He was mainly inspired by hunting scenes, ports, beaches, winter landscapes and, above all, pastoral scenes. His works were highly appreciated during his lifetime. One of his best canvases is in the Hermitage Museum: *The Hunters' Halt*. Other works include: in Amsterdam, *Winter Landscape Outside Haarlem* (1647); in Antwerp, *The Return from Pasture*; in Dresden, *Landscape with Shepherds* (1659); and in Munich, *Mountain Landscape*. He had numerous pupils, among them Pieter de Hooch.

Bol, Ferdinand (1610-1680)

Dutch painter, designer and engraver, born in Dordrecht, died in Amsterdam. As a very young man he went to Amsterdam and worked there under the guidance of Rembrandt, and they became firm friends. He was the best of all the master's disciples, and the one to feel his influence most directly. He married twice and had two sons. His early canvases are vigorous, with clever colouring; his masterpiece, *Portrait of the Four Governors of the Lepers' Hospital*, dates from this period. Later he was somewhat spoiled by success and too numerous commissions; his canvases became badly finished. His spirited engravings are first-class works, often as good as Rembrandt's. The Louvre has his *Mathematician*, the *Young Dutch Prince* and *The Philosopher*. The Amsterdam Museum has his *Self-portrait* and his *Portrait of Admiral de Ruyter*.

Bor, Paulus (called Orlando) (d. 1669)

Dutch historical painter, born in Amersfoort. In 1638 he was apparently at Honshobredijk Castle near The Hague, and in 1655 he became a member of the Amersfoort Guild. In that town can be seen his large family picture containing thirteen people.

Brouwer, Adriaen (*c.* 1605-1638)

Dutch painter and engraver, probably born in Haarlem, died in Antwerp. His life was a series of lost opportunities, wasted talents, heavy drinking and poverty, but he is conversely claimed to have been a noble character who rejected worldly splendour and despised riches. His mother, a Haarlem dressmaker, arranged for him to have lessons from Frans Hals, and he, taking advantage of his pupil's talent, worked him without respite and treated him very badly. Brouwer ran away to Amsterdam where his gifts were recognised. Then he went to Antwerp where he was accused of spying and thrown into prison, but was released on Rubens' intercession. In 1631 he was accepted by the Guild of St Luke in Antwerp, and Van Dyck painted his portrait. In 1634 he became a member of the society called The Violet. He died of the plague at the age of thirty-two. Both Rubens and Rembrandt owned several of his pictures. His canvases, superbly coloured, depicted mainly Dutch interiors with peasants drinking, smoking and playing. They surpass the best work of Teniers, who was, incidentally, his pupil. He was an admirable painter, combining imagination with Flemish verve and Dutch firmness of technique. His pictures can be found mainly in Dutch, Belgian and German museums. He also made several engravings. His *Sleeping Peasant* is in the National Gallery, *Peasants playing Cards* in Munich, and *Tavern Brawl* in Brussels.

Cano, Alonzo (1601-1667)

Spanish painter, sculptor and architect, born in Granada. In all three disciplines he displayed extreme talent, and the universality of his great genius enabled him to play an important role in the Spanish art of his period. He was the son of a sculptor and reredos-maker, and studied first with his father, then with Francisco Pacheco and Juan del Castillo, who taught him painting. He studied sculpture with Juan Martinez Montanès. He settled in Seville and had considerable influence there, almost equal to Velasquez' in Madrid. There he made the altar in the Church of Lebriga (finished in 1636) and the altar screens in the Church of Santa Paula. He was obliged to flee Seville after a duel, and went to Madrid where his intimate friend Velasquez welcomed him enthusiastically and got him appointed painter to the King. He spent thirteen years of intense artistic production in the capital. In Valencia he painted seven pictures for the Carthusian Convent of Porta Coeli, then returned to Granada in order to become a priest, obtain a living, and end his days in security. Endowed with a bizarre and violent nature, accustomed to lawsuits and quarrels, absurdly generous, Cano made art the dominant preoccupation of his life. His sculptures, preserved in churches in Seville, Córdoba, Granada and Madrid, are remarkable for their vigorous design and delicate colouring. In painting his work was considerable, including: *St Agnes* in the Berlin Museum, *Madonna in Adoration* and *The Crucifixion* in the Prado, and *St Anthony of Padua* in Munich. His teaching made Granada an eminent artistic centre.

Cocteau, Jean (1889-1963)

French poet, writer, dramatist, film-maker and painter, born in Maisons-Laffitte, died in Milly. Author of poems: *Opéra* (1927), *Clair-Obscur* (1954); novels: *Thomas l'Imposteur*, *Le Potomak*, *Les Enfants Terribles*; essays: *Essai de Critique indirecte* (1932); plays: *Les Mariés de la Tour Eiffel*, *La Machine infernale*, *L'Aigle à deux têtes*; films: *Le Sang d'un Poète*, *Orphée*, *Le Testament d'Orphée*. He is the author of works on painting: *Le Greco* (1943), and poems on painters: Bosch, Dali, Picasso, etc. Elected to the Académie Royale de Belgique and the Académie Française in 1955.

Coello, Claudio (1624-1693)

Son of a carver and pupil of Francisco Rizi, Coello was the last painter of the great 17th-century Spanish school. He was born and died in Madrid, where he painted pictures for the main altars in the churches of Santa Placida and Santa Cruz. He was a friend of the painter Carreño de Miranda who favourably influenced his technique, and of the architect Jiminez Donoso who worked with him on the designs and paintings for the triumphal arch and other decorations made for the arrival in Madrid of Queen Marie-Louise of Orleans, first wife of Charles II. In 1683 he painted frescoes in the dome of the Augustine College in Saragossa. In 1684 he returned to Madrid and was appointed painter to the King, Carreño's titles, duties and emoluments being assigned to him. In 1690 he inherited in addition the title of painter to Toledo Cathedral. The following year, however, when Luca Giordano arrived in Madrid, all the favour Coello had enjoyed crumbled away. Seeing that he could not compete with his prolific rival, he abandoned his work and let himself die. His main works include: in the Prado,

The Apotheosis of St Augustine and a fine *Portrait of Charles II*; in the Hermitage, a *Self-portrait*; and in the sacristy of the Escorial, the altar-painting *The Miraculous Host*.

Cotan, Sanchez (1561-1627)

Spanish painter, born in Orgaz, died in Granada. He specialised mainly in Madonnas, flowers and still-lifes. He studied in Toledo with Blas de Prado, then entered the Carthusian Order. First he painted Passions of Christ and flower-crowned Madonnas for the Carthusian Convent of Paular, then in 1612 he went to Granada and painted the historical subjects which decorate the four galleries of his monastery's cloister. In 1623, in Seville, he painted a *Virgin of Good Success* for Saint Augustin's Convent. A *Still-life* by him can be seen in the Granada Museum.

Dobson, William (1610-1646)

English painter and engraver, born and died in London. He was the pupil of Robert Peake and, later, of Francis Kleyn. Van Dyck came by chance on one of his pictures and, interested, desired to know the artist, whom he discovered in extreme poverty. Van Dyck very generously helped him out of his difficulties and recommended him to King Charles I, who commissioned him to paint portraits of himself, his son, and several important persons. During the Revolution, Dobson was thrown for some time into a debtors' prison. Of all the painters of that period, he came closest to Van Dyck. His portraits are excellent reproductions of nature. The National Gallery has a *Self-portrait*, and portraits of *Sir Harry Vaine* and *The Poet Francis Quarles*; Hampton Court has portraits of two men. One of his best works is the historical picture *The Beheading of St John* at Wilton.

Dou, Gerrit (1613-1675)

Dutch painter, born and died in Leyden. Son of a glazier, he attended Rembrandt's school in Amsterdam for three years. He made his career in Leyden. He concentrated first on portrait painting. He is certainly the most painstaking of all the Dutch painters who applied themselves to faithful rendering of the simplest domestic scenes. Not a detail escapes him, and he paints the most varying objects with exceptional and minute attention. Dou, to a great extent, shared Rembrandt's taste for the picturesque and the charms of *chiaroscuro*. He was highly admired both in his own time and the 18th century. In the Louvre can be seen his *Dropsical Woman* in which a doctor examines her "humours", a frequent subject with the lesser Dutch masters; *The Tooth-puller* in which certain critics recognise Rembrandt's father; *The Bible* and *The Old Woman* clearly influenced by Rembrandt; and the *Old Man reading*. Other pictures include *The Young Mother* (The Hague), *Young Woman at the Clavichord* (Dulwich), *The Evening School* (Amsterdam) and a quantity of night effects. He produced altogether about 200 pictures.

Dujardin, Karel (*c*. 1622-1687)

Dutch painter, born in Amsterdam, died in Venice. Certain points in his biography remain obscure. In his youth he visited Italy and Rome, where he was highly admired. Despite this success, he returned to Holland about 1655, having married a very rich widow from Lyons, whom he later abandoned. In 1656, at The Hague, he was one of the founders of the Society of the Pictura. His work was very painstaking, and he could not keep up with the orders that flowed in. He painted family scenes, portraits, landscapes and animals. In 1672, still missing the Italian sun, he returned to Rome and revived his old friendships and habits; he settled in Italy for the rest of his life. His paintings include: in the Louvre, *The Italian Charletans* and a *Crucifixion*; in Vienna, *Shepherd and Flock*; in Basle, *Bugler on Horseback*; and in Antwerp, *The Five Governors of the Antwerp Hospice*.

Elsheimer, Adam (1578-1610)

German painter, known also as Adamo Tedesco, born in Frankfurt, died in Rome. He studied with a pupil of Grünewald, through whom he absorbed the influence of the Dutch landscape artist; towards the end of the century he went to Venice then on to Rome. The effect he had on certain Roman painters must have been profoundly revolutionary. He skilfully assimilated Caravaggio's principles while remaining very original in his paintings, drawings and etchings, which to a surprising degree anticipate Rembrandt in style. He is the author of small mythological and religious pictures such as *The Flight into Egypt* (Munich Pinakothek), *The Good Samaritan* (Louvre), *Philemon and Baucis* (Dresden Museum) and *St Christopher* (Kaiser-Friedrich Museum, Berlin). The greatest number of his drawings are at Frankfurt in the Städel Museum. Elsheimer's works, all very small and executed with much care, were very much admired and sought after during the artist's life. He loved night effects and placed his pictures in beautiful Roman landscapes which anticipate the best works of Claude Lorrain. Elsheimer was the master of Pieter Lastman, himself the master of Rembrandt. Taking into account his direct collaboration with Saraceni and the skill of certain of his pupils, it is difficult to compile an accurate catalogue of his works.

Fischer von Erlach, Johann Bernhard
(1656-1723)

Austrian architect, born in Graz, died in Vienna. Son of a sculptor. From 1680 he made a long visit to Italy where he absorbed the influence of Borromini. About 1690 he worked as architect on the construction of the Castles of Frain (Moravia) and Engelhartstetten, and the Imperial Mausoleum at Gray. In 1693 he worked for the Archbishop of Salzburg: Klesheim Castle, Trinity Church (1694-1702), the church of St John's Hospital (1699), the Ursuline Church (1705), and the Collegiata (1696-1707), an original construction which represents Fischer von Erlach's first notable contribution to the problem of building to a central plan. Until the Archbishop's death in 1709 he retained the direction of Salzburg building. At the same time he held the post of architect-in-chief to the Austrian court. In Vienna he built the Strattmann-Windischgrätz Palace (begun about 1683 and completed twenty years after the artist's death), the Schönbrunn Palace, and Prince Eugen's Palace, today the Ministry of Finance (1695-1710), a rigid and austere building as demanded by its situation in a narrow street. In Prague he built the Gallas Palace inspired by the German Schlüter; in the Transton Palace his style displays its maturity and classicism. The Church of Saint Charles Borromeo, which he began in 1715, was finished after his death. Towards the end of his life he constructed the Imperial Library (begun in 1722), the Imperial Stables and the wing of the Chancellery in the Hofburg for the Vienna court. The numerous decorations of his earliest works denote Borromini's influence. Then his art improved, and French architecture, which he admired, influenced him to design increasingly classical works. He was the greatest and most influential architect in Austrian Baroque.

Greco, El (Domenicos Theotocopoulos)
(*c.* 1547-1614)

Spanish painter, born in Crete, died in Toledo. He came from a probably well-off family, and received a refined education. He was a solitary by temperament, independent, melancholy and proud; he desired both rich pleasures and spiritual development. He went to study in Venice, where there was a Greek colony numbering 4,000, and became the pupil of Titian who, with Michelangelo, Tintoretto and Bassano, influenced him greatly. He left for Spain, perhaps summoned by Philip II, and settled permanently in Toledo, making occasional journeys to Madrid and the Escorial. He wrote in addition to painting, and was very fond of music. His painted œuvre was enormous and he died leaving 200 started pictures. He signed his canvases in Greek characters. He decorated the convent of San Domingo de los Silos, Toledo, where he was eventually buried. Toledo Cathedral Chapter commissioned from him *El Espolio* and *The Sharing of Christ's Raiment* (1574). The Cathedral sacristy has twelve portraits of Apostles and *Christ giving his Blessing*. In 1579 Philip II ordered for the Escorial *The Martyrdom of St Maurice and his Companions.* The Church of San Tomás, Toledo, possesses his most famous picture, *The Burial of Count Orgaz*, which was ordered for it in 1584. In 1587 he made three painted altar-screens for San José, Toledo. The Prado has his *Baptism of Christ*, *The Resurrection*, *The Virgin ana the Apostles*, *The Holy Family*, etc. The Louvre has *Christ on the Cross.* He painted numerous versions of *Mary Magdalene, St Francis of Assisi, St Jerome, St Bernard* and *St Veronica*, a *View of Toledo* and a number of portraits, *The Poet Góngora*, *Head of a Dominican*, *Cardinal de Quiroga*, etc. His life remains shrouded in obscurity, and his work is somewhat enigmatic. His pictures have a mystic realism, and are characterised by audacious elongation of forms. He was accused of "lunacy" by his contemporaries and by 19th-century critics, but the 20th century restored him to a place in the front rank of Spanish art.

Hals, Frans (1580-1666)

Dutch painter, born in Mechlin, died in Haarlem. He lived in Haarlem and was the pupil of Karel Van Mander until 1602. He married and had a son in 1611. His wife died and he remarried in 1617 and had several children. His life was somewhat disorganised; he ran up numerous debts, and in 1662 he obtained support from the Municipal Authority; he died in a home for old men. At the age of thirty-six he painted his first group portrait, *The Banquet of the Officers of the Civic Guard of St George* (1616, Haarlem Museum). About 1621 he painted the marvellous *Portrait of a Man and Wife* (Rijksmuseum, Amsterdam). In 1627 he painted the second *Banquet of St Joseph* (Haarlem) showing a dozen officers in sumptuous uniforms with large white ruffs and admirably drawn faces. In 1633 he painted *The Repast of Officers of the St Adriaansdoelen*, a clever, vigorous and decorative picture and the chef-d'œuvre of the large multiple portrait compositions so popular with the Dutch at that period. In 1641 he painted *The Governors of St Elisabeth* (Haarlem Museum); the faces are boldly modelled against their white Puritan collars. In 1664 Hals was eighty, and passed the remainder of his life in the old men's home; as a mark of his gratitude, he painted the portrait of *The Six Governors of the Old Men's Home* and that of *The Five Governesses of the Old Men's Home*

(Haarlem Museum), both masterpieces. Altogether he painted about a hundred portraits and family pictures. He concentrated on faces, hands, officers' rich uniforms and beggars' rags. His most famous portraits are various figures of a *Laughing Boy* (Glasgow, Dijon, Schwerin, etc.); *The Young Singers* (Cassel); *The Jolly Toper* (Rijksmuseum, Amsterdam); *The Young Fisherman* (Musée des beaux-arts, Antwerp); the hideous *Malle Babbe, the Witch of Haarlem*, her mouth twisted in a horrible smile (Berlin and Lille Museums); *The Beautiful Gypsy* (Louvre), with laughing eyes and her chemise slipping to display her breast; the admirable *Descartes* (Louvre); *The Beresteyn Family* (Louvre), each head in which is astonishingly lifelike; *Nicolaes Hasselaer and his Wife* (Rijksmuseum, Amsterdam); and *Child and Nurse* (Kaiser-Friedrich Museum, Berlin).

His skilful brush gave spirit to the most ordinary faces. He is the painter of reunions of civic guards, and cheerful fellows making merry. All his models came from Haarlem, which he hardly left.

Holbein the Younger, Hans (1497-1543)

German painter, born in Augsburg, died in London. He and his brother Ambrosius were both pupils of their father, Holbein the Elder. In 1514 the two brothers went to Basle where they found work as draughtsmen with a printing firm, and Hans made about 300 engravings. At the age of twenty-seven he painted the *Virgin and Child*, and at twenty-nine the portraits of Jakob Meier and his wife (Basle Museum), which proved his immense talent as a portrait painter. He became intimately connected with Erasmus, and at that period produced numerous canvases, including one *Portrait of Erasmus* (1523), now in the Louvre, and another now in Basle, and the admirable *Meier Family Madonna*, now in the Darmstadt Museum. He was also commissioned to decorate several houses in Basle and the Council Chamber of the Town Hall. When he left for England, following the religious quarrels raging in Basle, Erasmus recommended him to Thomas More, who made him very welcome. He painted portraits of *Nicolas Kratzer* (1528) and *Sir Guilford* (1527, Windsor Castle). Returning to Basle, he bought a house on the Rhine, and painted a portrait of his wife and two children (Basle Museum), but the religious climate there was too much for him and he rapidly returned to England and settled in London in 1531. In 1534 he painted the *Portrait of Thomas Cromwell*, then Henry VIII's Master of the Jewelhouse. From 1536 he was one of the King's painters. That year he painted the *Portrait of Sir Richard Southwell* (Uffizi). In 1537 he painted *Jane Seymour* (Vienna) and *Lady Vaux* (Prague). In 1538 he went to Belgium to paint the *Portrait of Christine of Denmark* (National Gallery), a masterpiece of grace. Other portraits include *Anne of Cleves* (Louvre), *The Duke of Norfolk* (1540) and *John Chambers* (1542). At the height of his great powers he was killed by the plague. He was undoubtedly one of the greatest painters in the world.

Laer, Pieter van (d. 1642)

Dutch painter of Italian landscapes and popular scenes, nicknamed Il Bamboccio. He came from a rich family, studied with Elsheimer, then, when very young, went to Rome and stayed there sixteen years. Poussin, Sandrart and Claude Lorrain became his friends, and the Duke of Alcala his patron. During this period he made numerous drawings round about Rome, and used them later as backgrounds for his pictures. He enjoyed painting fêtes, masquerades, fairs and festivals, and this seems to have given rise to his nickname. In 1636, he is known to have been studying in Rome under Johan del Campo. Subsequently he went to Vienna to work for the Emperor Ferdinand III; returning to Haarlem, he worked with Gerrit Dou. He then went to Nijmegen where he painted some portraits. In Holland, as in Italy, he was very successful. It is not known for certain whether he was drowned or committed suicide. His works are rare and very much sought after. They include: *Italian Peasants* (Dresden); *Self-portrait* (Uffizi); *Two Horses in a Stable* (Munich); *Shepherds* (Louvre) and *Peasant Scenes* (Vienna).

Lievens, Jan (1607-1674)

Dutch painter and engraver, born in Leyden, died in Amsterdam. He was the son of a tapestry-worker, and at the age of eight became the pupil of Joris van Schoten; then he worked for two years in Amsterdam with Pieter Lastman. He was very precocious, and by the age of twelve was already a good copyist. His earliest works resemble those of Rembrandt. At eighteen he had a reputation as an excellent painter. He spent several years in England and took the opportunity to make portraits of the royal family; many of his pictures from that period are today attributed to Van Dyck. In 1632 he returned to Leyden; two years later he joined the Antwerp Guild, and he married in 1638. In 1642 he painted *The Continence of Scipio* for the town of Leyden. The Elector of Brandenburg and the Stadtholder Frederick Henry were his patrons. In 1643 he was back in Amsterdam; in 1661 he went to The Hague, and in 1671 he painted the ceiling of the hall of the Estates-General. After a life of luxury he died in poverty. He did several altar-pictures for churches in the Low Countries. Other works include *Portrait of Vondel, the Poet* (Amsterdam), *Portrait of a Young Boy* (Berlin), *The Visitation* (Louvre) and *St Peter* (Rotterdam).

Murillo, Bartolomé Esteban (1617-1682)

Spanish painter, born in Seville of a modest working-class family. When his father died he was brought up by his uncle, a surgeon, and at the age of ten he entered Juan de Castillo's studio in Seville. The departure of his master in 1640 left him without resources, so in order to live he sold religious pictures at the fair. He left for Madrid where, thanks to Velasquez, he worked at the Buen Retiro, the Alcazar and the Escorial. In 1645 he returned to Seville. The Franciscans commissioned him to paint a series of pictures for their convent (*St Thomas of Villanueva giving Alms*, Seville Museum; *The Angels' Kitchen*, Louvre; *San Diego with the Beggars*, Prado) and these established his reputation. They show the influences of Zurbarán, Ribera and Velasquez, and display a very personal poetic feeling. The painter employs the most ordinary ingredients of everyday life and, simultaneously, the supernatural. In 1648 he married Doña Beatrix de Cabrera, of noble birth. At that time he painted *The Immaculate Conception with a Monk writing about the Mystery* for the large Augustine cloister in Seville, and an admirable *St Anthony of Padua* (1649) for the baptist chapel of Seville Cathedral. In the second part of his career, from 1652, his harmony became purer and his technique more free. He successfully interpreted languorous ecstasy, celestial visions, martyrs' triumphs, and tenderness of the Infant God and the Immaculate Conception. This was the period of *The Ecstasy of St Francis* (San Fernando Academy), *The Adoration of the Shepherds* (Prado), the *Virgin of the Chaplet* (Louvre) and the famous *Little Beggar* (Louvre). From 1615 to 1680 the painter produced without pause. In Seville he decorated the chapel of Saint George of Charity with superb and vast paintings, also the convent chapel of the Capuchins-without-the-walls. In 1665, still in Seville, he painted two of his most admired canvases for the church of Santa Maria Blanca: *The Patrician's Dream* and *The Dream Revelation* (now in the Prado). At this period his palette lightened: *Girl offering Flowers* (Dulwich College, London), *Old Woman Spinning* and *Galician Woman counting her Money* (Prado) and *Mos Muchachos* (Pinakothek, Munich) are significant examples. In 1680, in Cadiz, while he was working on *The Mystic Marriage of St Catherine of Siena* for the Capuchins, he had a stroke. He went back to Seville where he died two years later.

He produced a considerable body of work always on very few themes. He painted numerous *Immaculate Conceptions*, each one with its own individual charm. The Mother of Christ holds a special place in his work (*Virgin of the Rosary*, Prado; *Virgin of the Chaplet*, Louvre). He made numerous representations of the Infant Jesus and St John. He interpreted episodes from the Old and New Testaments with great naturalism (*The Prodigal Son*, Prado). Lastly, he painted numerous saint figures: *St Elisabeth of Hungary tending the Scurvied* (Prado); *St Anthony of Padua* (Seville). When he painted beggars and homeless children he was resolutely naturalistic. Sincere piety seems the dominant trait in his character, and early widowerhood made him very unhappy. His life was entirely devoted to work. All his harmoniously coloured pictures show consummate skill and bear the stamp of Andalusia.

Pacheco, Francisco (1564-1654)

Spanish painter, writer and poet, born in Sanlucer de Barrademo, died in Seville. He was the pupil of Luis Fernandez. He held an important position among the Sevillian painters because he was entrusted, in 1598, with the decoration of Philip II's funeral monuments. In 1600 he painted *Scenes from the Life of St Raymond* for the Convent of Mercy. In 1603 he painted the picture *Icarus and Daedalus* for the Duke of Alcala. He opened a school of painting attended by Velasquez who, in 1618, became his son-in-law. His important works include: *The Last Judgement*, 1612, for the Convent of San Isabel; *The Baptism of Christ* and *Christ served by Angels*, 1620, for the College of San Hermangilde. After 1625 he concentrated almost exclusively on literature and in 1649 wrote a work on the art of painting. Characterised by severe mysticism, his philosophy of art leaves nothing to the painter's inspiration. Though deputed by the Inquisition to see that orthodoxy was maintained in pictorial work, he was popular, his studio serving as a meeting place for all the fine wits of Seville.

Pozzo, Fratel Andrea (1642-1709)

Jesuit, born in Trent, died in Vienna. After his novitiate he studied painting. He began by decorating the chapels of his order. As his reputation grew he decorated other churches in Italy. The Austrian Emperor Leopold summoned him to Vienna, where he worked until his death. His works are in Dresden, Florence and Nantes museums.

Ravesteyn, Jan Anthonisz. van (*c.* 1570-1657)

Dutch portraitist, born and died at The Hague. He was probably Mierevelt's pupil. After a visit to Italy, he lived for some time in Delft, then at The Hague, where in 1598 he was admitted to the Guild. He was one of the founders of the Pictura and had numerous pupils. The Hague Museum holds his principal pictures, all fairly large, and depicting assemblies, civic guards and portraits.

Rembrandt (Harmenszoon van Rijn) (1606-1669)

Dutch painter, born in Leyden, died in Amsterdam. He was the fifth of a family of six children of a Leyden windmill proprietor. In 1620 he began studying in the Academy there, but he had such a gift for drawing that he was soon apprenticed to the Leyden painter Van Swanenburg. In 1623 he left for Amsterdam and worked with Pieter Lastman, pupil of Elsheimer. Shortly afterwards he returned to his native town, where he was quickly surrounded by disciples. About 1630 he went to live in Amsterdam; as soon as he arrived he was fortunate in getting a commission. This was *The Anatomy Lesson of Professor Pietersz. Tulp* (1632), now in The Hague Museum. The perfection of the portraits in this picture earned him many more commissions. Man of the world and fashionable painter, Rembrandt was lionised everywhere, and in 1634 he married Saskia van Uylenburch, the ravishing daughter of a rich merchant; he loved her tenderly and frequently painted her, once dressed in a marvellous gown (1633, Cassel), again as a dazzling *Danaë* (1636, Hermitage), and as *Susanna Bathing* (1637, The Hague) and *Flora* (London). It was a period of success, fortune and happiness, though saddened by the deaths of three of Saskia's four children. Titus, the only survivor, died at the age of twenty-seven, before Rembrandt himself. Captain Banning Cocq employed him to paint his company for the Arquebusiers' Corporation; begun in 1640, this has become famous as *The Night Watch*. At the same period he painted some Biblical pictures: *The Angel Raphael leaving the Family of Tobias, Samson threatening his Father-in-law* (1635, Berlin), *Christ's Passion* (Munich) and *The Holy Family* (Louvre). But Saskia died in 1642, and Rembrandt withdrew to the country, probably to Elsbroech, where he began to paint landscapes, flowers, shell-fish and so on: *Landscape with two Bridges* (Eindhoven) and *Three Trees* engraved in 1643. This retreat from public life, following the whirlwind of success he owed to his talent and his marriage, deepened his depression. He lived with a gentle young peasant woman, Hendrikje Stoffels, for several years before he married her in 1656. The *Susanna* (1650) in Berlin, the *Woman Bathing in a Stream* (1654) in London and *Bathsheba* (1654) in the Louvre show us what she was like. His sumptuous tastes, however, and a certain disdain for material considerations brought him at last to poverty, if not to complete bankruptcy. In 1656, however, he received a commission from Professor Deijman for *The Anatomy Lesson of Professor Johann Deijman*. The self-portraits of his later years give more evidence of his internal misery than of his money worries. His genius became more and more vast and profound with *The Combat with the Angel* (1659, Berlin), *Moses breaking the Commandment Tablets* (1660, Berlin) and *St Peter's Denial* (Amsterdam). In 1661 he received his only official commission for the Town Hall, Amsterdam. After long discussion he was granted the task of one of the lunettes. He painted the *Conspiracy of Claudius Civilis*, but it was refused on the grounds that the proportions were bad. To sell it, at least in fragments, Rembrandt mutilated the unrecognised masterpiece. He became more and more lonely. Hendrikje Stoffels died in 1662, Titus in

1668. His last six years are marked by the predominance of mystery and the supernatural: *St Matthew* (1660, Louvre), *The Return of the Prodigal* (Hermitage), and *The Syndics of the Cloth Guild* (1661). A *Self-portrait* (1668, Cologne) and *Ruth and Boaz or the Jewish Bride* still show his splendid colouring. His output was immense: besides his, at least, 350 paintings, he made a great number of absolutely beautiful engravings. This marvellous artist is probably one of the greatest and most profoundly poetic painters of all time.

Ribalta, Francisco de (1551-1628)

Spanish painter, born in Castellon de la Plana, died in Valencia. He served his first apprenticeship in Valencia, then went to Italy to study the works of Raphael, Sebastiano del Piombo, Correggio and the Carracci. Back in Valencia he was much admired, and the Archbishop Juan de Ribera commissioned him to paint a *Last Supper* which formed part of the remarkable series of paintings he did for the college of Corpus Christi. He also decorated several churches. He was the first master of the Spanish school to make *chiaroscuro* the main ingredient of his work. He trained many pupils, including Ribera. The Prado houses his *St Francis of Assisi* and *Christ's Body borne by two Angels*, but the majority of his canvases are in the Valencia Museum.

Rottenhammer, Johann (1564-1625)

German painter, born in Munich, died in Augsburg. He made his early studies with Donauer, then, while still very young, went to Rome, where his little historical pictures were much admired. In Venice he studied Tintoretto and Veronese; here he lost some of his heaviness and acquired enough elegance for certain of his works to be attributed to Caliari. In Venice he decorated churches in the town, and the Duke of Mantua gave him commissions. He went to live in Augsburg, protected by the Emperor Rudolf II, for whom he painted a *Banquet of the Gods*, considered one of his best works. Jan Brueghel and Paul Brill sometimes helped him to paint the landscapes in his pictures. Canvases by him are in Munich: *The Judgement of Paris*, 1605; in Berlin: *Arts*, *Poetry*, *Music*, *Painting and Architecture* and *The Holy Family* with a landscape by Jan Brueghel.

Seghers, Hercules (*c.* 1590-*c.* 1638)

Dutch painter, evidently born in Haarlem, died in Amsterdam. His life is little known. In 1617 he may have been the pupil of Gillis de Coninxloo. In 1613 he is found as a member of the Haarlem Guild. In 1640 he married Anneken van den Brugghen. He lived successively in Amsterdam, The Hague and Utrecht. He almost certainly went to Italy and Montenegro. Tradition has it that he was a drunkard, and died after a serious fall. His pictures, mainly landscapes and animals, were much admired by Rembrandt. Some of his engravings are in the British Museum and the Bibliothèque Nationale, Paris, and some of his pictures are in the Amsterdam and Berlin museums.

Somer, Paul van (*c.* 1576-1621)

Painter of the Flemish school, born in Antwerp, died in London. In 1604 he worked in Antwerp, then went to Amsterdam, where he and his brother Bernard painted numerous portraits. In 1600 he was in London, and in 1617 in Brussels, where he painted the portraits of Albert and Isabella. Most of his works may be seen at Hampton Court and in the National Gallery, London.

Spranger (Bartholomeus van den Schilde) (1546-1611)

Painter of the Flemish school, born in Antwerp, died in Prague. Son of a rich Antwerp merchant, he displayed a marked talent for painting while very young. He studied with Jan Mandyn, then Frans Mostaert, and, about 1565, in Paris with Marc Duval. He subsequently went to Lyons, Milan and Parma, where he worked with Bernardino Gatti, a disciple of Correggio. He spent three years in Rome painting the Villa Caprarola for Cardinal Farnese, and *The Last Judgement* for Pope Pius V. Appointed first painter to the Emperor Maximilian in Vienna, he was made painter of the Imperial chamber in 1584 and given a title in 1588. He returned to the Low Countries in 1602, then went to Cologne and Prague where he ended his career. Most of his paintings are in the Vienna Museum.

Steen, Jan (1626-1679)

Dutch painter, born in Leyden. Son of a rich brewer, he very early manifested exceptional gifts. He was almost certainly the pupil of Nicolas Knupfer, Adriaen van Ostade and Jan van Goyen. In 1648 he was one of the founders of the Leyden Guild. In 1649 he married van Goyen's daughter and they had six children. He stayed in The Hague until 1654, then ran a brewery in Delft until 1657. After spending some time in Haarlem he returned to Leyden in 1669 where he kept an inn, and remarried in 1673 to Maria van Egmont, a tripe-seller by trade and a widow with two children. He led an insecure life and after several financial catastrophes was obliged to sell some of his pictures for a very poor price. Tradition paints him as a drunkard because a great number of banquets figure in his work. This is untrue. He was a law-abiding citizen and the honest father of a family; he worked intently and painted a great deal, studying reality with care and reproducing the surroundings familiar to him. The atmosphere in his pictures is sometimes that of cheerful bohemianism; he also depicted tavern scenes: *The Libertine* and *The Parrot's Cage* (Amsterdam). *The Family Meal* (Louvre) is very gaily turbulent. The *Feast in an Inn* is a cheerful romp. Full of roguery, he was a profound observer, and his taste, lighting effects and rich colouring make him one of the best little Dutch masters. He left over 500 pictures which hold important places in museums.

Ter Borch, Gerard (1617-1681)

Dutch painter, born in Zwolle, died in Deventer. He was a pupil of Pieter Molyn in Haarlem, and while very young drew views of the town and the surrounding countryside and scenes of military life. He travelled extensively: to London in 1635, and probably to Italy, Amsterdam and Münster in 1645. He was in Münster when the final treaty of the Thirty Years War was signed. He seized on the occasion to gather in one canvas the portraits of all the plenipotentiaries (*The Treaty of Münster, 1648*, National Gallery, London). The admiring Spanish Ambassador took the artist to Madrid, where he was well received by Philip IV. He went to London, and lived for some time in Paris. He returned to Holland in 1650, settled in Deventer, married, and lived rich and respected. He became the town *burgemeester*. He was a personal and independent artist, and his pictures are very informative about contemporary life and habits. He was a marvellous observer and a pleasant genre painter. He depicted violent incidents like brawls, or sophisticated little scenes with military gallants and young ladies decked in rich satins. His drawing is accurate and lively, his painting light, refined and colourful. His best works include: *The Music Lesson, Soldier showing Gold Coins to a Young Woman* (Louvre); *Trumpeter bringing a Message, Cottage Interior* (Munich); *Young Lady washing her Hands* and *Lady in a Satin Dress* (Dresden).

Ter Brugghen, Heindrik (1588-1629)

Dutch painter, born in Deventer, died in Utrecht. He worked in Abraham Bloemaert's school in Utrecht. He lived for ten years in Rome and Naples and painted numerous canvases for churches and private individuals. When Rubens went to Holland he judged Ter Brugghen to be one of the best painters in the country. His works include *The Four Evangelists* (Deventer), *Christ before Pilate* (Copenhagen) and two pictures in the Cassel Museum.

Tristan de Escamilla, Luis (1586-1624)

Spanish painter, born near Toledo, died in the same town. He was one of the first eminent disciples of El Greco, whose style he absorbed to the extent that a picture signed by him was attributed to El Greco. He displayed a precocious talent, and at the age of thirteen painted a series of pictures for the Yepes church. Many of his canvases may be seen in the churches of Toledo and Madrid. He was a remarkable portrait painter: *Cardinal Sandoval, The Bishop of Toledo* (1619), *Lope de Vega* (Hermitage). He also painted a *Last Supper* for the monks at Las Sisla, near Toledo. A large number of his works are in the Prado including *St Jerome* and *Portrait of an Old Gentleman*. Velasquez much admired his work, and Tristan was a link between El Greco and Velasquez, and the precursor of the brilliant Spanish school of the 17th century.

Valdés-Leal, Juan de (1622-1690)

Spanish painter, sculptor, engraver and architect, born in Seville. Pupil of Antonio del Castello. His wife and two daughters were painters like himself. In 1660 he was one of the founders of the public academy of drawing in Seville, about which he and Murillo had some disagreement, although they were intimate friends. When Murillo died Valdés-Leal became the greatest master in Andalusia. He left a considerable body of work, particularly in Seville. His striking colouring, firm drawing and powerful imagination make him a painter of the first rank. He explored dramatic effects and preferred violent subjects: executions, martyrdoms, the ugliness of death; the *Two Bodies* in the Hospital de la Caridad, Seville, is a canvas of horrific realism. His principal works include the paintings in the church of the Hospital de la Caridad: *The Triumph of the Cross*; *The Story of the Prophet Elijah* and *The Martyrdom of St Andrew* in the church of San Francisco, Córdoba; and *The Assumption* in the National Gallery. The Prado has only two of his pictures. He also engraved historical subjects and portraits.

Valkenborch, Lucas van
(before 1536-1597)

Painter of the Flemish school, born in Mechlin, died in Frankfurt. He depicted genre scenes and landscapes and executed miniatures. In 1560 he was a pupil and in 1564 a master of the Mechlin Guild. A Protestant by religion, he took part in the revolts against the Spaniards, and had to flee his native town in 1566. After a stay in Antwerp, where it is thought he studied with Pieter Brueghel, he fled to Aix-la-Chapelle, then to Liège, then to Frankfurt. In 1570 he went to Linz on the invitation of the Archduke Matthew. In 1595 he worked for the Archduke Ernest. He seems to have stayed for a long time in Nuremberg. There are numerous pictures by him in Brunswick, including a *Landscape*; in Frankfurt, including *View of Antwerp* and *Cows in the Pasture*; and in Vienna, including *The Four Seasons*, 1580, and *The Deer Hunt*, 1590.

Velasquez, Diego Rodriguez de Silva y (1599-1660)

Spanish painter of noble Portuguese origin, but whose family had been in Andalusia for two generations; he was born in Seville and died in Madrid. When very young he began painting with Francisco Herrera the Elder, then with Pacheco, whose daughter Juana he married in 1618. About 1619 he painted *The Adoration of the Shepherds* and *Christ in the House of Martha and Mary*, both in the National Gallery, and both clearly showing the influence of Ribera. In 1622 he went to Madrid where he painted a *Portrait of the Poet Góngora*, then went back to Seville. The following year he went again and entered the service of Philip IV in the capacity of valet; he was appointed the King's painter after his first portrait of *Philip IV* on horseback and in armour which won him a complete triumph. After that he painted *Don Carlos, The King's Brother*, and *Juana Pacheco*, his own wife. From that moment Velasquez never ceased to grow in stature as a painter, as a court dignitary, and as the friend of the King. He then began a series of *Royal Hunts*, of which only *The Boar Hunt* in the National Gallery, *The Deer Hunt* in Lord

Ashburton's Collection in London and *The Group of Cavaliers* in the Louvre survive. In 1628 he met Rubens who was on a diplomatic mission to Madrid; his picture *Los Borrachos* owes something to the Flemish master. In 1628 he made his first voyage to Italy, visiting Venice, Ferrara, Bologna and Rome, where he spent a whole year. There he painted two studies of the Rome gardens (now in the Prado); in Naples he painted a *Portrait of Doña Maria*, Philip IV's sister, *Joseph's Tunic* and *The Forge of Vulcan*. From 1631 to 1636 he worked almost exclusively on royal or noble portraits. They form a grandiose series celebrating the Spanish court: *Prince Don Balthazar Carlos* (Florence), *The Prince aged six* in a little hunting costume, *Philip IV* in hunting dress, *Prince Don Fernando* and the *Equestrian Portrait of Balthazar Carlos* (all in the Prado). Apart from his *Christ on the Cross* (1638), there were only more portraits: *The Duke of Modena* and *Admiral Pareja* (National Gallery), *Don Antonio Pimentel* and *The Count of Benavente* (Prado); this series of portraits ended with *The Surrender of Breda* (1647, Prado), a celebrated canvas, and the only other historical subject he treated besides *The Expulsion of the Moors*. In it he shows himself a most sombre colourist and a master of harmony. Apart from princes and princesses, one finds hardly any other portraits but of invalids and idiots, because the King, wishing to forget his own misfortunes, surrounded himself with dwarfs and fools. The Prado houses: *El Primo*, *The Child of Vallecas*, *The Idiot of Coria*, *Sebastian de Morra*, *Pablillos de Valladolid*, *Antonio el Inglès* and others. In 1649 he made a second journey to Italy, sent by the King to study the creation of a fine-arts academy and to purchase pictures for the royal collection. There he painted the famous *Portrait of Pope Innocent X* (Palazzo Doria), and the even more famous *Toilet of Venus*, known as *The Rokeby Venus*, in the National Gallery. On his return in 1651 the King loaded him with favours and appointed him steward marshal of the palace, a post which made him responsible for the whole internal running of the royal household. He painted the *Infante Felipe Prosper* and the strange symphonic works *Mariann of Austria* (Prado), and *The Infanta Margarita*. He also finished *Las Meninas*, a marvellous technical achievement. Nothing is harder to define than the genius of Velasquez, which reached its height when he was fully mature. He produced less when he was tired by the functions and duties of his position. *The Holy Hermits* and *The Tapestry Weavers* are his last masterpieces. In 1659 he was made a Knight of Santiago and became increasingly intimate with Philip IV. He organised the sumptuous celebrations to celebrate the marriage of the Infanta Maria Teresa to Louis XIV. The responsibility was a heavy strain, and he died six months later, having earned a magnificent funeral. He was the most powerful and most original painter of the Spanish school.

Vermeer of Delft, Jan (1632-1675)

Dutch painter; almost nothing is known of his life, except that he was born in Delft, married and had two children, and died at the age of forty-three. He was scarcely recognised in his time, and even less in the next century. For a long time his pictures were attributed to other painters. His skilfully diffused light, his cold, silver-grey colouring and his fine observation make him one of the greatest painters of all time. Throughout his work the atmosphere is quiet and discreet and his figures use calm gestures. His interior scenes express the warmth of family life in their harmonious colouring and luminous prospects. His townscapes and landscapes express a rarely equalled depth of feeling.

His most famous pictures include: *Street in Delft* and *The Kitchen Maid* (Amsterdam), *Woman with a Pearl Necklace* (Berlin), *The Courtesan* and *Girl reading a Letter* (Dresden), *View of Delft* (The Hague) and *The Lacemaker* (Louvre).

Vroom, Hendrik Cornelisz. (1566-1640)

Dutch landscape and seascape painter, born in Haarlem. When very young he lost his father, who was a sculptor. His mother remarried with a porcelain painter, Cornelis Hendriksen, from whom Vroom received his early education. He started by painting townscapes. He visited Spain and Italy. In Rome, under the auspices of the Medici Cardinal, he met Paul Bril who greatly influenced him. After his stay in Italy he went to live in Paris. Returning to Haarlem he painted numerous religious subjects with the intention of selling them in Spain. He embarked for Seville, but was shipwrecked on the coast of Portugal and took the opportunity to paint some sea scenes; he liked these subjects so much that he went on using them all his life. Lord Nottingham commissioned him to do the cartoons for the famous tapestries celebrating the destruction of the Armada; they have since been burned, but engravings had been made from them. This commission necessitated a visit to England, during which his portrait was painted by Isaac Oliver. In 1616 he is mentioned as a member of the Antwerp Guild. His works include: *Naval Battle at Gibraltar* (1607) and *The Y outside Amsterdam* in Amsterdam, and *Rowing Boat* and *The Arrival of Leicester at Flushing in 1586* in Haarlem.

Witte, Pieter de (1548-1628)

Painter and sculptor of the Flemish school, born in Bruges, died in Munich. He studied in Italy. He was an intimate friend of Vasari, who employed him on his work in the Vatican, probably in the Sala Reggia. The Grand Duke of Tuscany most probably gave him commissions after Vasari's death in 1574. He painted some pictures for the Palazzo Pitti. Maximilian of Bavaria invited him to the Munich court, where he ended his career. He designed the mausoleum of Louis I of Bavaria (Our Lady of Munich) and the statues in the Munich Residence. The Ariana in Geneva houses his *Religious Ceremony*, and the Vienna Museum *The Holy Family*, *St Ursula* and *The Fall of the Angels*.

Wright, John Michael (*c.* 1623-1700)

Portraitist of the English school, born in Scotland, died in London. He was a pupil of Jameson, and left Scotland to go first to England, then to Italy. In 1648 he was appointed a member of the Florence Academy. Returning to England, he soon ranked alongside Peter Lely as a portrait painter. In 1686 he accompanied Lord Castlemaine's embassage to the Pope. On his return, his reputation was eclipsed by Kneller's. His works include *The Actor John Lacy in Three Roles* (1675) at Hampton Court, and *Thomas Hobbes* in the National Portrait Gallery.

Zuccaro, Taddeo (1529-1566)

Italian painter, born in Sant'Angelo in Vado, died in Rome. He was a pupil first of his father Ottavio, then of Pompeo da Fana. At the age of fourteen he went to Rome to pursue his studies in Vitto's studio. He specialised in portraits and historical subjects. He acquired the protection of the Duke of Urbino, who asked him to do a series of frescoes in Urbino

Cathedral. In Rome, he was employed successively by Popes Julius III and Paul IV. He did some paintings in Cardinal Farnese's villa at Caprarola. He died very young, undermined by work and excess, and was buried in the Pantheon next to Raphael. His *St Mary Magdalene transported to Heaven* may be seen in the Pitti Palace, Florence, and *The Dead Christ* in the Galleria Borghese, Rome.

Zurbarán, Francisco (1598-1663)

Spanish painter, born in Fuente de Cantos, died in Madrid. His parents were simple peasants. When very young he went to live in Seville and worked a two-year apprenticeship with Pedro Villanueva. He was influenced by Caravaggio and made friends with Velasquez. Despite early success with the decoration of the San Pedro chapel in Seville Cathedral, he left in 1625 and went to live in the little village of Llerena, in Estremadura, where he married and had several children. His fame was such that in 1629 the Seville authorities invited him to return to the capital. He painted four canvases on *The Life of St Bonaventure*, now in the Louvre and the Dresden and Berlin museums. In 1629 he decorated the Church of San Pablo and painted *The Visions of St Peter Nolasco* for the convent of Merced. He also did the admirable paintings which may still be seen in the Church of the Magdalena, Seville, and the series for the Carthusian convent of Las Cuevas, now in the Seville Museum, with *The Virgin Protectress of the Carthusians* and *The Repast of St Hugh*. His talent was recognised; he was appointed official painter to the town and loaded with commissions. In 1631 he painted *The Apotheosis of St Thomas Aquinas* (Seville Museum), one of his most admired works. Between 1633 and 1638 he undertook the decoration of the Car-thusian convent at Jerez, from which come the pictures now in the Grenoble and Cadiz museums. From 1638 to 1640 he carried out the cycle in the Guadalupe monastery, a gigantic and flawless work. It comprises sixteen pictures, mainly depicting episodes in the life of St Jerome. He also celebrated other male and female saints: *St Casilda* (Prado), sumptuous and thoughtful, with make-up on her face; *St Catherine*, *St Lucy*, *St Inez*, *St Eulalia* (Seville, Louvre, Prado), nearly always noble ladies with heavy brocade robes. From 1640, Zurbarán went through a great crisis; his wife died, he remarried, had numerous children, and experienced an obscure and difficult period. He left Seville and went to Madrid where he could count on Velasquez' friendship. The King tried to attach him, but despite royal favour he progressively faded out. In 1650, however, he painted the great founders of religious orders for the convent of the Capuchins of Castellon at Córdoba. Another series of holy founders may be seen in the San Fernando Academy. Also in 1650, Philip IV charged him to decorate the Buen Retiro; the theme suggested, *The Labours of Hercules*, is in striking contrast with the artist's personality. In 1661 he painted an *Immaculate Conception* (Budapest Museum) and a *Christ laying aside his Garments* (Church of Jadraque). His later works lost power. Perhaps he was deeply affected by the brilliant rise of a new painter, Murillo. He died in Madrid. He remains one of the most astonishing painters ever. He had melancholy, great simplicity, and unique honesty. He painted only in response to a deep compulsion. When he lost faith in himself he stopped working, and his life is marked with periods of absolute silence. Nicknamed the "Spanish Caravaggio", he was the most ardent painter of Spanish mysticism.